The Journey: Sunrise

Copyright © 2017 by Dominic Herron. All rights reserved. This book or any portion thereof may not be reproduced or used in any manner whatsoever without the express written permission of the publisher or writer except for the use of brief quotations in a book review, or social media post, with proper credit given to the author.

The Journey: Sunrise

Mr Goodlow,

Thank you for all the support and wisdom over the years. Believe it or not, but our time together helped shape me and definetly helped contribute to the lessons in this book. I wish you continued health & happiness. Enjoy!

Dominic Herron

A Guide To Your Own
Peace & Happiness

Additions by Tracey Edwards, Liscenced Clinical Therpist MSW

The Journey: Sunrise

This book is dedicated to the lives I have touched,
and who have touched my heart as well.

Thank You.

The Journey: Sunrise

Contents

1. Sunrise 15
2. Every Journey Begins With A Step 21
3. Open Your Heart To The Possibilities of A Better Life 31
4. Law of Attraction 35
5. Personal Responsibility 41
6. Balance 47
7. Companionship 53
8. The Life You Have Built: Is It Really You? 61
9. Fighting To Stay The Same 67
10. Mirrors 77
11. Nothing Grows Without The Warm Rays of Love 83
12. Given Permission To Be Bigger 89
13. Doing The Work 101

The Journey: Sunrise

-Introduction-

Welcome to The Journey: Sunrise! I'm happy that life has brought us here together. This book presents various topics that are focused on bringing you closer to your own heart, and achieving personal happiness and joy in life! Every topic is presented in a simple, yet intuitive fashion, so that the information is easy to digest, but thought provoking in nature. Because of this, I recommend reading each chapter, and thinking or meditating on the parts that resonate most with you for a bit. There are pages after every chapter for jotting down the things that really hit home, or elicit strong feelings. These are the things that require the most attention on your Journey. Take a day or two to think about why they meshed with you, and try incorporating positive alternatives to any struggles you might uncover into your daily life or mindset. This text is a very reasonable length, done purposefully so that you can re-read it over again as needed. Not everything in this book you will agree with, and not everything will resonate, but the things that do, even if they are uncomfortable, should be considered, discussed, and meditated on. They are your roadblocks, stopping you from moving forward on The Journey. Talk to people about them and see how others respond, and the dialogue that ensues. Take your time with the content. This is not a road map, simply a guide on your Journey to your own love and peace. Enjoy.

The Journey: Sunrise

Preface
by
Tracey Edwards, MSW

The definition of 'life' is the sequence of physical and mental experiences that make up the existence of an individual. The definition of 'journey' is an act or instance of traveling from one place to another. These two words sum up our existence. This life's Journey can be stunningly beautiful, or equally as ugly. We traverse many ups and downs. These experiences mold and shape us. They define us, and change us. But in the end, we all must grow. For with no growth, there is no life. With no journey, there is no new perspective. Change is the only thing certain on our Journey. Forever looming like the ever-present seasons. Our old ways must die off like autumn leaves, only to sprout new beginnings and a new chance at life in the spring. This book is your starting point to a better you. Regardless of how much we change or grow, this life's 'Journey' is our story, and our mark left on this the world. Make it a good one.

The Journey: Sunrise

-1-

Sunrise

Wake up. It's morning now. You've been asleep far too long. There is so much you've missed. So much to see now that you're up.

You are reading this book, so it is safe to assume that you are here for a reason. A reason you probably don't even understand right now. That's great! This book will give you a deep understanding of a lot of your fears, emotions, ideals, and norms in your life, with the simple theory that you cannot start to remedy a problem if you don't know it's there. Simply put, happiness, and peace, start on the inside. These pages will help to untangle the web of information embedded into your psyche. It will likely challenge you in a lot of ways. Just know that this life is your Journey. Everybody has a different path they have traveled on, and different paths for the future. Everyone is here to learn their own lessons. This book is based on my personal Journey. These are the things I realized and helped me get to a real place of happiness. A real place of love. And a real place of peace You can take

The Journey: Sunrise Penned By Dominic Herron

The Journey: Sunrise

these things and build on them, or disregard them. Either way, life has brought us here together, in this moment, for a reason. One thing about the Journey you are about to start, is that there are no right or wrongs. There is no magic pill or answer. It starts inside you. And you are 1 of 1. So uniquely beautiful. Your Journey is just as distinctive. So pack your bags, and most importantly, open your heart. Your Journey awaits!

Lets define what "The Journey" is. I started to refer to my state of mind as 'The Journey' after a really hard and stressful break up. I was dating my High School sweetheart for over 8 years. We got married halfway through that time, but decided to call it quits after 4 years. Amical, but painful nonetheless, as one can imagine. During the beginning of this time, I did what most people do after a difficult break up or similar stressful situation, and began to find outlets to deal with the emotional pain. Parties, liquor, staying busy with work, isolation, defensiveness, and quickly getting into a new relationship, were my coping mechanisms. Emotional pain does a lot to our psyche. More on that later. I unknowingly indulged in any and everything, to not have to deal with the emotions and thoughts. Soon, though, I slowly began to realize that none of this was filling the emotional void. In other words, I still wasn't happy. For moments, I felt great, on top of the world, free to do as I please. But I always had to come home and face myself. I tried to avoid that as much as possible. Most of us do. Some longer than others. After some time I finally began to sit still. Literally and figuratively. I began to realize that true happiness, contentment, and love, doesn't come from any source outside of ourselves. No thing, event, or person can give us real inner peace. The problem is, everything outside of us is temporary. Our spouse? Sickness, accidents, or a change in said person can take them. Our bank accounts? Unforeseen economic failings can wipe them out. Our possessions? Well, time will break down anything. Our lifestyle? Once again injury, disease, or economic activity can wipe that out as well. There is only one thing that is unchanged during all of these examples. You. Your heart, soul, and mind. So if you can be at peace, no matter what happens to you or your surroundings, your level of appreciation and contentment can stay the same. Obviously emotions and feelings can fluctuate from time to time, but having a base, or median level of joy, means you will only fall so much, before your inner peace catches you. 'The Journey' is about you becoming everything you think you need. And by picking this up and reading this far, it's safe to say, you are on that path.

The Journey: Sunrise

What is on your mind?

The Journey: Sunrise

-2-

Every Journey Begins With A First Step

The one and only purpose of the The Journey, is to get to know yourself. Why? Because like any relationship, it is impossible to deeply love someone without first getting to know them. Unlike a relationship, you are stuck with you forever (scary, right?). There is no divorce, or bad break up. You and your heart, soul, and subconscious are forever linked. We have to get to know ourselves. There is no magic answer in these pages, YouTube videos, or seminars. The answers lie inside you, but finding them can be the hard part (and where these tools come into play). Understanding one's self and inner thoughts and workings, helps us attain whatever it is in life that we truly want.

One thing that can really help is to simply ask ourselves 'Why' to many of the things we do. Ask yourself 'Why?' to a question about something we do or think often. About 6-8 times. Here's a an example of a conversation with a friend. An example that shows although we think we understand why we do things, it is often a much deeper decision then we realize. And you can ask yourself the same.

Me: What is your ultimate end goal for going to work everyday?
Friend: Well, money.
M: Why?
F: To pay bills.
M: Why?
F: To live comfortably.
M: Why?
F: To free up time.
M: Why?
F: To pursue my passions.

Often what we really want, gets lost in translation for a variety of reasons. This can be busy schedules, focus on money, cultural norms, parental influence, peer pressure, and many other factors. My friend was working to eventually pursue his passions, not realizing it. Well couldn't he pursue them now? Or course! Even though his schedule was filled with his 'day job', his passion (in his case teaching others), was still possible to pursue, even for a few hours a week. Pursuing a passion naturally adds a greater purpose, joy, and in some cases, financial freedom to our life, as people tend to pay for passion! He felt as if at a certain financial number, or a certain number of hours of freedom, he could then pursue his dream.

The Journey: Sunrise
Penned By Dominic Herron

Find Your
Passion

Well this is simply the 'carrot on a stick in front of the rabbit' analogy. This 'number' may never come, and as a result, he may never pursue his passion. The world loses out on an amazing teacher, because of an unnecessary financial barrier, placed in his own mind. This is the case for many of us. We may feel that at a certain 'number' happiness will come. This is the number one source of anxiety and stress, feeling as if we are not supposed to be where we are. We can completely ignore what we do have, and how far we have come, constantly looking into the future. Today is valuable. Today can be the day we move towards our passions, and away from our 'number'. Today is the day to start your Journey to happiness, peace, and patience. *I'm happy to say he is now well on his way to pursuing teaching, and a lot more fulfilled because of it!*

While getting to know yourself on a deeper, more subconscious level, a lot of potential struggles, contradictions, aspirations, goals, and more, might bubble to the surface, allowing you to figure out the purpose behind your actions. Why is it important to recognize these things? Well the reasons are plentiful. Here are just a few.

We don't realize it, but the human experience is one of culture, and groups. We naturally tend to form groups, or packs, and within those develops a culture, or a norm, if you will. Sociologists consider culture as the

formation of traditions and trends that link humans in a common group. Therefore, human 'culture' existed, throughout history, even in prehistoric societies. For example, ancient Romans were not to lay eyes on the naked body of their new wives directly after the marriage ceremony. Wouldn't go over so well with men in our Western culture, now would it? The Spartans, who were known for their homosexual relationships, when getting married, had their wives shave their heads and wear men's clothing, to ease into heterosexual relations. Not exactly how things work now, huh? These are extreme examples of how cultures vary throughout history, or how 'normal' varies throughout history.

The Journey helps us to sift through cultural norms, and find out who we really are and want, and not what we've been programmed to be. Digital marketing experts estimate that most Americans are exposed to as much as 4,000 to 10,000 advertisements each day. EACH DAY! With such a bombardment of people trying to convince of things, we can easily get caught up in someone else's ideology of us. The point is: If we don't have sight of ourselves, we will follow someone else's vision of us. Think of it this way, the CEO of Apple would love nothing more then to see you outfitted with all of their newest gadgets and gizmos. So they advertise heavily to attract you to their products. Is that what you really want? Is it what all your friends have, and so you would feel left out if you

My Greatest Enemy Is My INNER ME

The Journey: Sunrise
Penned By Dominic Herron

-Lupe Fiasco

didn't?

Simple questions, that never get asked of our self-conscious, or '**Ego**'. Your Ego is the part of the mind that mediates between the conscious and the unconscious, and is responsible for reality testing, and a sense of personal identity. Essentially, your Ego takes your subconscious thoughts, and puts them into real life situations, emotions, fears, and other feelings that we can consciously understand. Getting to know yourself on a deeper level, or an Ego level, means finding out what you really want out of life, and thus attaining a happiness that a new iPhone, or lack thereof, can't give, or equally, take from you.

Another reason getting to know yourself is vital, is because until you are comfortable with who you are, you will attract people who are not familiar with themselves either. Let's break it down a bit. Not knowing who you are, at an Ego or self-conscious level, as we discussed, can greatly affect our everyday decisions. The same is true for relationships. Why are you really attracted to this person? What makes you click with each other? What are your motivations for being with this person?

Until we know ourselves, on a deeper level, a lot

of our decisions could be based on emotions that we are unaware of. For example: abusive relationships. Why do people get into these, and more importantly why do they stay? The answer is in the subconscious. See most of these situations involve people who were never really given the unconditional love they needed in childhood, so as they get older, they desperately seek this love. Conversely, controlling and domineering individuals, with their own set of childhood problems, see another's desperation as an opportunity for control, or to get their own needs met. They are also looking for love, in a completely different manner. One willing to do anything for love, the other taking it by force. Both of these individuals have motivations for their behavior. None are positive. The motivations are based on needing someone or something outside of themselves, to feel loved or validated. Getting to know your Ego, helps to understand these motivations, finally breaking the cycle of abuse, and other potentially damaging behavior in relationships or personally.

Lastly, getting to know your Ego, helps you attain true happiness! As we discussed earlier, delving into the subconscious can help us determine what our motivations, desires, and dreams truly are. It helps to rid us of our actions that are based on lacking something, or needing a 'thing' or someone. It frees our minds and hearts to reach their potential, and grow, steadfastly, any way they please. This is true happiness. Freeing ourselves of the notion that we need things or people to be content. Enjoying every single day, with an honest and content outlook, not always looking to tomorrow. Exploring our creativity and passions, free of insecurities and fear. Our Ego often holds us back from these things, and opening it up can help us to always move forward, in the most genuine way possible, and with love and acceptance in our hearts. True feelings of contentment, power, confidence, and love!

What is on your mind?

-3-

Open Your Heart to the Possibilities of A Better Life

This part of The Journey frustrates a lot of people, and really held me up for a long time as well: **most of us need to see things to believe them.** We need proof. We need assurance. We need concrete evidence that makes sense to us. Although absolutely understandable, this is mostly from the fear of our Ego. Anything new or different equals danger, and death to who we have become. For example, if our subconscious has a defense or dislike built up to a certain religion because of what we have been told since childhood, then learning more about that religion can be scary. Talking with people of that faith may anger you in frustration, and turn you away. But this is only because your Ego believes that if you change your viewpoint on this one thing, you will, for all intents and purposes, die. For so long, this viewpoint was who you were, and if that changes, you are no longer you. Our Ego can oftentimes be our biggest obstacle.

"My greatest enemy is my inner me".

Writer/musician Lupe Fiasco once said.

But if there is one thing The Journey has taught me, is that some things in life simply cannot be understood until after they happen. For example, try explaining love to someone who has never experienced it. How about describing how your favorite food tastes. Maybe what the air near a beach, or in a forest smells like. See, often in our life, we experience things that can never really be grasped until the experience happens. There simply is not the right set of words in the English language that can describe a feeling, or experience. The Journey is no exception. Nobody will be able to describe what true self-love feels like. Or what freedom from social and cultural norms feels like. They won't be able to accurately describe how it feels to not act out of fear or insecurity. And they will not be able to give a satisfactory answer to how much more secure you will feel inside yourself on The Journey, especially when your security is not based on relationships, jobs, or anything else outside of you. You simply have to do it to experience it. You have to make positive, healthy changes, more than likely, fighting yourself most of the way through. You have to do the work. Ego doesn't like change, but growth is

The Journey: Sunrise

only attained through it. Ultimately, you had to get on a roller coaster for the first time to feel that feeling. The key is to believe in yourself. That you are good enough. That you are love, and loved. That you are special, and you don't need anyone, anybody, or anything to still look in the mirror and love what looks back. But ultimately, you have to be willing to sit, and strap yourself into this theme park ride called The Journey. You won't fully understand, nor appreciate the benefits, standing on the sidelines. But once you do, you'll will look back at the obstacles you conquered and be proud, and excited for another round!

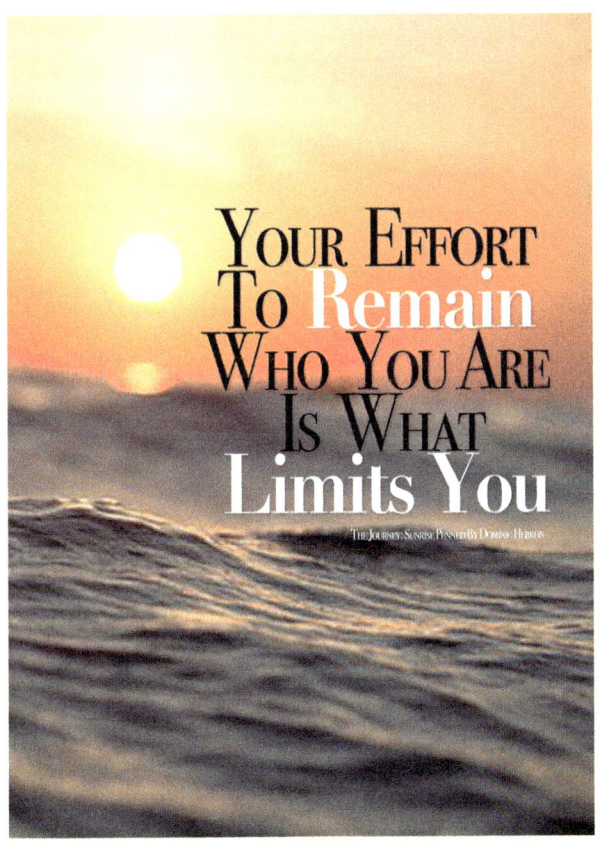

What is on your mind?

-4-

Law of Attraction

The law of attraction is massively important to understand along the Journey to personal contentment. It is so important because it dominates our day to day lives, and drives almost every circumstance that comes our way. The Law is seen as similar to the Law of Gravity, or other laws that govern our human existence here on earth. Plainly speaking, there is no escaping it. The Law of Attraction is the ability to attract into our lives whatever we are focusing on, both the negative, and positive. The Law of Attraction uses our mind and thoughts, to translate whatever is in those thoughts, into reality. To put it very simply, our thoughts turn into physical things or situations eventually. If you focus on negative things, you will remain under those effects, attracting or noticing things and situations that also match your thoughts. This could mean jobs you don't like, unhealthy relationships and friendships, drug abuse, certain health problems, or simply noticing the person across the room chewing loud, or being upset with traffic. Alternatively, If you focus on positive things, and have goals and ambitions in life, you will more than likely find a way to achieve them through your drive for those things, all while noticing and appreciating the positive things in your life like health, family, shelter, or just a sunny day or warm night.

This Law is what supersedes our subconscious thoughts. What does this mean? Well if our subconscious is plagued with fear, insecurity, or guilt, then naturally our thoughts may tend to be more negative. Our view of the world might be one of "full of bad people", or we might not expect amazing things in our life. These thoughts and feelings are then applied through the Law of Attraction, becoming what we focus on, and thus draw into our lives. A great example of this is Social Media, and in particular Facebook (the News could be applied as well). This example (along with another I will explain), helped me realize the power of The Law of Attraction. I once held a conversation with a friend who said there was too much negativity on Facebook. Fights, breakups, sad stories, celebrity news, etc. At the time, I wholeheartedly agreed with them, citing all of the craziness I had seen. When I learned about the Law of Attraction, I changed my mind frame to things more positive. I began to try to look at things in a better light than before. So what did I start to see as I scrolled? Things that my negative mindset would

never have seen: a ton of positive stories! Giveaways, students, scholarships, community news, marriages, funny videos of animals and children, all things that were positive. I began to not even notice the negativity. This happened simply because when I chose to put out (and thus focus on) more positive energy, I attracted (or noticed it) a whole lot more! I was further convinced with this example. Think of your dream car.

What make and model is it? Color? Really picture it in your brain. Now that you have it there, notice how many times you will see it in the near future. It might astonish you. The Law of Attraction is based upon a simple fact that what we focus on, we notice more. We draw towards it, we see it more often, in other words, we ATTRACT it.

It is so important to grasp even the basic concept of the Law of Attraction. It can affect so many things in our lives. Most of the time, we are behaving or thinking certain things on a subconscious level, and thus we are attracting them. If we are angry or unhappy in a job or relationship, even the slightest thing can set us off. Why? Because of the negative mindset we are in. We notice (attract) and amplify any and everything bad, possibly ignoring any positivity about the situation. This is why information about The Journey, and a path to understanding your psyche is important. But in the same breath, we have a very real, very conscious control over our perceptions of things. Take a situation like your job, and begin to find things you like about it. Same with a living situation, or body image for example. Your job might fund your lifestyle. Maybe it paid for dinner with a friend last night. Your body may not be where you want it to be, but people still love you. Maybe you shouldn't be so hard on yourself. Your mom might annoy you, but maybe she gives you insight, and unconditional love. These are merely examples of how slowly making small, but important, changes in your perception, will then draw more positive things into your life. You will notice and enjoy so much more, no matter your situation or environment. There is a ton of information on the Law of Attraction, and it would require a whole book to scratch the surface, but understanding the principals can help you make real life changes, both in mood and circumstance.

Live Life Without An Audience. Social Media Gives Everyone A Stage. Choose to Perform For Yourself.

The Journey: Sunrise by Dominic Herron

What is on your mind?

-5-

Personal Responsibility

This is probably the biggest single step you can take on The Journey. The step on the path of **personal responsibility**. This revelation started me on my Journey, and continues to fuel my steps. You see, most people spend most of their lives deflecting blame onto anything outside of themselves. I broke up with my ex because THEY were crazy. I lost my job because my BOSS was a bitch. My PARTNER treats me like shit. These are some of the common complaints I hear day in and day out. Complaints filled with reasons why we act the way we do, or feel the things we do. Reasons outside of ourselves, that we feel are either bigger than us, or out of our control. The first step to personal responsibility is to realize the universe generally gives you back exactly what you put out into it.

The Law of Attraction is a great concept to get to know. This really hit home while having a conversation with a friend of mine. He was complaining about his mate being selfish. Upon a little digging, I found out that the reasons he got with her in the first place, were mostly for his own gain, not hers. There wasn't an exchange of love, passion, and unselfishness, just a 'what can they do for me?' motivation. Although there were genuine feelings involved, the relationship was ultimately started for selfish reasons by him. And now, the selfishness was being turned back on him, and he didn't like it. The simple lesson here is that sometimes, we only focus on having the things we want, not realizing how our actions and thought processes impact other people. When you give selfishness to people, it's only a matter of time before you get it back. But when we take personal responsibility for how we act, feel, and most importantly, our intentions, we begin to understand how our actions affect others. Selfish intentions, leads to selfish people being in our life. After all you can only attract what you are.

When we act, or feel an angry or sad emotion about a situation, it is important to ask ourselves "What were my intentions when starting this, and how have my actions brought about this outcome?" Asking this deflects the blame from an outside source, and forces us to take responsibility for certain outcomes of a situation, including good or bad ones. It is important

to reflect on ourselves, because after all, as much as we'd like to convince ourselves otherwise, we are the only thing we can control, and thus most circumstances are actually self inflicted.

I have been in conversations where the other person gets very angry while making a point. Emotional, defensive, and unreasonable. I'm sure most of us can relate. Even in this situation, we can try to take personal responsibility. Even if what is being said is completely against our beliefs, or is coming from an unreasonable person, we can still OWN our response and reaction. I simply took it as a lesson to work on my own patience, looking inward and controlling what I could, my emotions. Instead of letting my impatience or frustration consume me, I tried to understand why their response was angering me, and not making me want to be patient with them. I also tried to think about how I could have approached things differently in the future, even a little.

You can only get better from taking personal responsibility. This is the beautiful thing about it, and why it is so important. If you can understand your own role and decisions in any situation, good or bad, it ONLY leaves room for improvement. You will be forced to figure out what you could have done to not have this happen again (or for it to continue to happen in a positive situation), and in this thought process, will come up with solutions that will only better yourself.

THE JOURNEY: SUNRISE
PENNED BY DOMINIC HERRON

THE HARDEST THINGS TO SAY ARE USUALLY THE MOST TRUTHFUL. THE HARDEST THING TO DO IS TO ADMIT THEM TO YOURSELF.

When we deflect blame or point the finger, even in situations where we might not be the person mostly at fault, or situations that are truly out of our control, we stop growing. This places a reason, outside of our own thoughts and emotions, as to why we behave the way we do. This keeps us in the same place, with the same mindset. If we can look in the mirror for everything that happens to us, we can find ways to improve and ensure the situation does not occur again, or if it does, it will with a lesser amount of consequences. Even if the situation couldn't have been avoided at the time, we can avoid making the same mistakes that put us there. We can learn from our behavior, and avoid ending up in a similar situation again.

The Journey: Sunrise

What is on your mind?

-6-

Balance

Balance is one of the many ways we should look at nature and try to mimic it. Day and night. Cold and hot. Rain and sun. Prey and predator. Nature gives us so many examples of divine balance. We should strive to mimic these qualities in our day to day, and long term lives. The most common cause of stress and anxiety, is believing we should be somewhere or something we are not. We can sometimes visualize a place or salary we would like, and think about how happy we would be if we achieved that. But just as the trees wait patiently all winter to bloom again in the spring, we have to be patient while we work towards those things. We have to have balance. Balance your long term goals, with enjoying your day to day. Balance your energy between your relationship and yourself. Balance your day with work, and rest. The balance isn't always perfect, but maintaining a SPIRIT of balance helps us to be much more mindful, and appreciative in our daily lives. We can appreciate our long term goals, while also enjoying the road to the them. The reality is, we may not achieve our 'ultimate' goals due to health or injury etc. Our goals may shift, or become less of a priority as we travel along our Journey and change (starting families or moving our residences for example). If accomplishments are your only source of joy, you'll always be chasing happiness. After all, there will always be something to accomplish. This is never ending. We have to find balance, so as to enjoy the process, thus attaining happiness no matter where we are on our Journey, and living a much more peaceful, content life.

It is not always all or nothing. If you have a job and want to pursue your passion, it's possible to spend time doing both. If you want to work out more, but are pressed for time, maybe 5 minutes of stretching will do. You don't have to commit an hour to it to feel like you are accomplishing something. It's OK to have a cheat day on your diet. Again, balance. You do the absolute best you can, without feeling the pressure to do everything. That only leads to stress. I for example, after being diagnosed with a brain aneurysm, became obsessed with accomplishing my goals before I inevitably passed (in my head). This lack of balance lead to an extreme fear of death, also selfish behavior, fearing my goals would be left on the shelf. After mindfulness therapy, meditation, a lot of self work, and embracing balance in my life, I began

The Journey: Sunrise

to focus less on my goals, and more on enjoying working towards them. I focused less on all the people I could potentially help, and more on those that I already have. I focused less on the blessings I wanted in the future, and more on the blessings I had. I counted my cherished memories as much as I counted what was on my bucket list. This took my stress level to an all time low since the diagnosis, and has drastically improved my outlook on life, allowing me to accomplish more than ever! I focused less on what I didn't have and more on what I did.

You don't have to be something, or someone, to be working towards that. If you don't enjoy the Journey, your destination will never truly come. There will always be a new goal, and happiness will forever be in the distance. Law of Attraction will pull more positivity into your life when you have better outlook. You will enjoy the moments more, and be at your best all the time. Understanding that life is a Journey, not a race, can help you attain a sense of balance and peace. Don't rush the moments, they are all that we have.

...urney,
...on Will Never Truly Come.

The Journey: Sunrise by Dominic Herron

The Journey: Sunrise

What is on your mind?

Written With Love

-7-

Companionship

We are so indoctrinated in our current culture. You'd be hard pressed to watch a movie without a love interest, or to sit through a set of commercials that didn't include a couple of some sorts. We brag about relationships, show off how in love we are in Facebook posts, and often look down on those who are single, especially around holidays or events. We are surrounded by the message of, as Frank Sinatra put it, 'You're Nobody Until Someone Loves You'. We are as I call us, 'The Disney Generation'. Filled with hopes of finding 'The One' and living 'Happily Ever After'. While admirable, the first thing wrong with this concept, is that it teaches us that we have to find love outside of ourselves, not inside. That unless someone sees us as worthy, we are worthless. But when you live in a fairytale, anyone can be your Prince Charming. And there are so many people who wear that crown well. They say all the right things, and make all the right moves to sway you. But the problem with a Prince

Charming, is that they can only be a prince for so long. Eventually they have to become a king, and that is when he/she is exposed. See, similar to relationships, a prince's job is no more than a show of nationalism, meaning they just have to look the part. Being a great king/queen, though, is all about action, and nothing about appearance. Often times in monarchies, royalty could only marry other royalty. If they chose to marry someone not of their class, they could never bear the royal crown, and neither could their children. Similarly, if we are in a place of self love, or contentment, we should seek to find others in that same place. But it starts with us ascending to that *personally*, not looking for it in someone else, and not just looking the part. We have to find our own crown inside of us. Build and shape our own glass slipper. We will eventually get to the point of not SEEKING a 'Happily Ever After', and as such, the antics of those who only PLAY the role of Prince Charming, will not only not be effective, but frustrate them to the point that they stop trying. This effectively eliminates all the relationships that are not only unhealthy for us, but built on appearance only, with no substance.

Once again, the Law of Attraction keeps those without our same intentions and level of growth, out of the way. Being confident, self loving, and self assured, we won't be LOOKING for anything, and thus can see people for who they really are. We will be able to recognize a person built on identity, love, and self-awareness, and one built only on a shiny gold plated

crown.

Similar to the idea of a Prince Charming, we often get so caught up in titles and statuses in relationships, and in life period at times. I've heard a lot of folks state that if a man is serious, he'll give you a title. This line of thinking is why most relationships fail. This means that from the moment you meet a potential partner, you already have expectations put on their love. You have motivations and intentions, based on a title. But titles are just that, a name that describes something. While a title is great, what really matters is the actions of the person with that title. For example, you may have a male or female friend who treats you with respect, cares for you, accepts you for who you are, and has always been there for you. While on the other hand, you may know a married couple whose values have declined beneath respect and acceptance. The point is, regardless of the status of a relationship, how you're being treated and loved, from a genuine place, should take precedence over a title. After all would you rather have a lifelong, genuine friendship, or a temporary title? Those friends may eventually become a mate, but it should play out naturally, with no expectation. Doing this allows us to see and accept someone for who they truly are, not just who they are being in search of a certain status. It is important to do our best to see people for who they really are before we lock ourselves into a relationship.

Similar to the construction of a house, the best relationships are built on a strong foundation of friendship. Rush the foundation, and eventually the whole house will fall. Build a strong, solid base, and your structure will stand firm and tall. Your level of acceptance, love, and genuineness is your foundation. Seek others with the same level of compassion, and keep them in your life, regardless of status. If you are meant to be more, let it happen naturally. After all forcing a relationship with someone who you are not meant to be with, will fail eventually. The Law of Attraction will eventually place things in your life that are meant to be there, or remove elements not meant to. If you force something, you might be taking a temporary positive feeling, and exchanging it for a future disappointment. If it is meant to be yours, it will be. Trust that, and trust in yourself. Remember, The Journey is about being content in yourself and in every day of your life. Try to not overly fantasize about the future, and enjoy today.

A solid foundation takes time and patience to build. We often rush things to avoid temporary negative feelings such as loneliness or sadness. We may latch onto

We are all so desperate
[to] be understood, yet have never
taken the time to
understand ourselves.

[Lo]oking For Love Everywhere
But
[Not] In Our Own Hearts.

The Journey: Sunrise
Penned By Dominic Herron

people in our lives, usually mates, who although are not bad people, simply have not invested enough time and energy in us to love us like we think they do. We give them everything. Time, communication, emotions, experiences, and then claim they are the only ones who understand us. But what if we gave all of that energy to those who are on our "I know I can call when shit hits the fan" list? What if we fantasized about the perfect family or friendships, instead of the perfect relationship? This may be all the love we need to patiently wait, and build something genuine with a potential mate. Family, loved ones, and lifelong friends, these people are the people we should look to invest in. We have stock in our own Fortune 500 company, but choose to abandon it and invest everything in a startup instead. The startup company has limitless potential in our mind, and can go much farther than the established one. The thrill and excitement of something new is always dangerous to the heart. We can ignore the longevity and staying power of an established brand. Small businesses come and go; over 500,000 are started a month. Much like relationships, we have established brands that have been around for dozens of years. They have shown the test of time and continue to support you. Invest wisely. Even if you believe in the new thrill, the new company, continue to invest heavily in your own brand, your own company. Let the startup grow slowly, and steadily, understanding that until it reaches Fortune 500 status, you have to focus on what's important. It is the same with relationships,

romantic and otherwise.

Isolation in relationships is very common. We can potentially latch onto our lover, and begin to feel they are the only one in our corner, often exacerbating any standing issues or problems with family and friends. Suddenly we feel we can finally cut off seemingly toxic familial and friendship ties, because after all, we can go home to our only true friend. This presents numerous problems on our Journey. First, as we discussed, we cut off our established relationships for a new one. Second, we become even more dependent on that person for our own identity. After all, if we have no friends and family to talk to, we need that relationship to fill our natural need of human interaction. He or she and their life, becomes just as much a part of you, as you and yours, often building a dependency for things like validation, comradery, purpose, beliefs, and comfort. Through their family, friends, job, etc. you may feel like you have those things as well. But as we discussed, a dependency on someone for identity, inevitably leads to you losing yours. If you give yourself enough reasons to stay, even if you are unhappy, you inevitably will. The purpose of The Journey, is to get to a place of self sufficiency. Relationships should never be built on a NEED of someone, rather a solid foundation of loving someone for who they are and growing steadily together. This type of love ensures that everyday will be a give and take of love, and not filled with fear of losing it. But the first steps to loving anyone, is to find that love within you, and of yourself so that your love

What is on your mind?

-8-

The Life You Have Built: Is It Really You?

The seemingly important ideas of titles or relationships in our culture, is a great segway into another important realization: A lot of your ideas, thoughts, and theories are not truly your own. The idea of a title meaning a man/woman loves you, probably has not originated with you, but with a set of cultural and ideological 'norms', or conditioning. The same can be said for so many other beliefs that we hold dear. From religion, to politics, to sports teams, and even race relations, we have been given an identity since birth. So, how do we find out who we really want to be? How do we sift through the constant barrage of titles, labels, and ideologies? Well, the first step in any major change, is to be aware. Hopefully at this point in the book, your mind is open to new concepts, and to realizing that a lot of the wiring in your thoughts were due to outside influences, inherited since birth.

Knowing is half the battle. My favorite line from Fight Club was "Its only after we lose everything, that we aren't afraid to do anything". In the same vein, once we are open to re-sculpting our own values, ideas, and norms, we begin to 'lose' our old identity, one that was inherited or given to us. After we have erased our cluttered chalkboard, we can begin to fill it in from an honest, loving, and secure place, thus finding out who, and what we really are and want to be!

With real love-of-self replacing superficial ideas and norms, we will naturally start to understand that there is plenty of room for our differences. We will, after understanding and respecting our own flaws and inherited ideology, inevitably begin to feel the same for others. This makes us less judgmental, less angry, more patient, and most importantly, more loving of others because we will give them the same understanding and kindness that we have given ourselves. You might become curious as to how and why they believe what they do, wanting to delve into their subconscious (similar to understanding your own) instead of assuming, or judging. You might feel more connected to others than ever, because you realize we are all on the same Journey, we just have different paths. This realization has helped me tremendously in my relationships with others. No more arguing, or resentment. I simply try to understand them, offer advice or opinions based on my own Journey, and lovingly accept their reaction to

It's Less about The Destination, And More About Enjoying The Scenery Along The Way...

The Journey: Sunrise Penned By Dominic Herron

it. It is important to understand that we all have a deep seeded love for each other buried deep in our hearts, but since birth we have been given ideologies that may have divided us, or given us reason to not dig that love up. Understanding yourself better, and more importantly, giving yourself kindness for inherited ideologies, helps you shed feelings of self-hate, pity, guilt, or resentment, and helps you

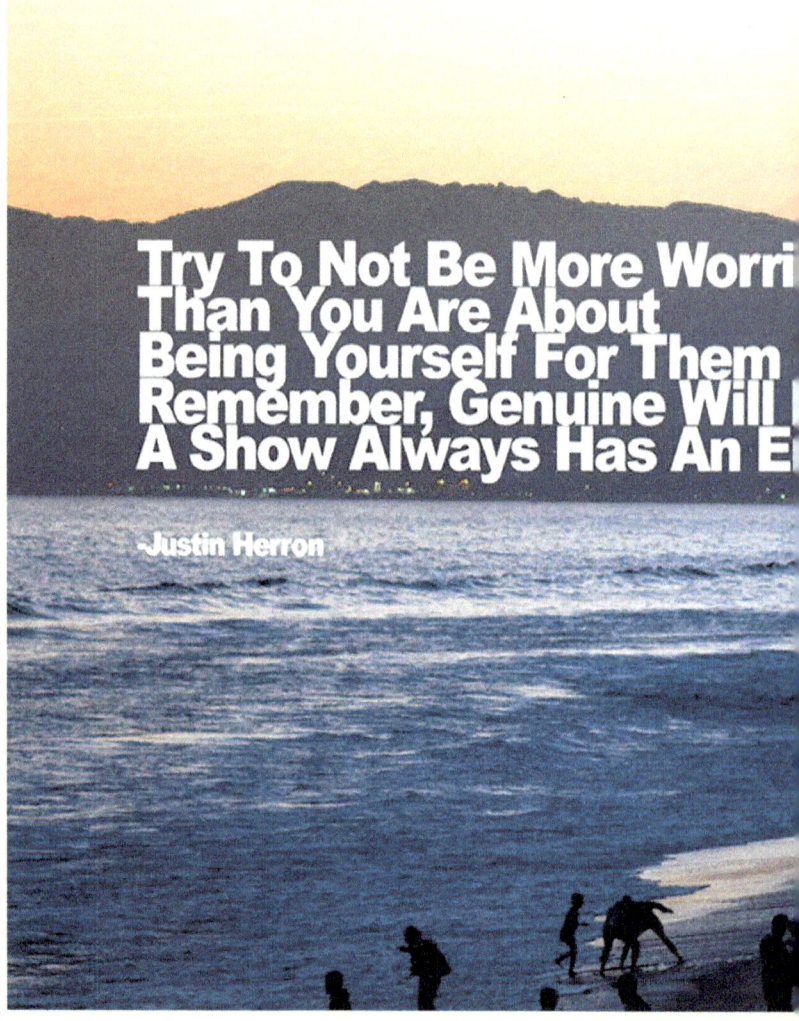

give that kindness back to the world, allowing them to do the same.

Again, let's give people more love than they have been given, or have given themselves, and allow them to unearth their self-forgiveness as well, shedding whatever feelings or ideology they have inherited, and tapping into that deep seeded love in their hearts!

What is on your mind?

-9-

Fighting to Stay The Same

I often have discussions with people about various topics on The Journey. And I'm sure you have had lively debates about certain topics. Often, because most of us have been conditioned, or are in an insecurity-based place, topics such as relationships, personal growth, self-love, spirituality, and childhood problems, often lead to a person getting defensive. Defensiveness, to a certain extent, in and of itself, is not a bad thing. Our Ego (or inner thoughts; self) often is fighting for survival. When survival is your main goal, anything new, or different is seen as threat. So when new ideas, thoughts, or patterns are offered, they are often met with harsh defensiveness. This is simply because people have lived in a fear-based place for so long, they are comfortable there. Again, understandable. But I realized, for myself, that whenever I was emotionally defensive (anger, frustration, fear) usually my defense was wrong, and the idea I was arguing against, was actually one worth

GENTLE SOUL,

YOU CARRY SO MUCH
BAGGAGE ON YOUR HEART

IT'S TIME TO GIVE THOSE
BAGS BACK TO WHO
THEY BELONG TO...

The Journey: Sunrise penned by Dominic Herron

exploring.

Again, our ego wants to survive comfortably. If someone tells us, for example, that we don't really love ourselves, even though the thought never really crossed our mind before, we might feel in that moment that we do indeed love ourselves. That might naturally lead to us going on the defensive. Not basing that thought on facts or experience, but simply because the idea that we might not love ourselves is too dangerous to entertain, for fear of losing our identity of who we have become, and thus, death to our ego. As I say: "You are fighting to stay the same". Anytime we get defensive, simply over a new idea, or criticism, instead of giving it careful thought and meditation, we are truly fighting to stay the same, with the same mindset and ideals. If after some self reflection, you simply disagree, that is amazing, and going to happen all of the time in life. But if we get emotionally defensive, something has probably opened a wound that we have ignored for some time. Don't fight the messenger, or the message. Instead, take what is being said and give it reflection. How can this conversation make you a better person? Even if it is just becoming a better listener, or maybe just being better at sympathizing with people, and understanding their unique perspectives. Instead of fighting to be the same, fight to grow. Fight to challenge yourself in every way and in areas that make you most uncomfortable. Fight for yourself.

The Journey: Sunrise

'as I call it:' "*Fighting To Stay the* SAME"

The Journey: Sunrise

I often use the example of a high school Junior. We all remember it well. Daily classes, relationships, gossip, friendships, dances, and basement parties. What if you were the same exact person now, as you were then? What if all the things that mattered most to you then, like your first 'love', clothes, gas money, prom etc, were what mattered now? Wouldn't be much fun would it? At a lot of points in your life, you grew. You came to accept new ideas, philosophies, dealt with loss, made mistakes, and fought for the wrong reasons, but learned the right lesson. In the same vein, who we are today is more than likely not who you will want to be in a decade. Allow yourself the same opportunities to grow and expand, understanding that you never have it figured out, as I'm sure the 16 year old you thought. You might look back at right now, the same way you look back on high school. Don't fight to stay the same, and don't fight the world, or the people in it. Fight your yourself to never fight the wrong battles, and instead, win the war of wisdom. Be your own hero.

Most people spend their lives building walls, to keep people out, instead of doors to let people in. But if we begin to give people the chance to love us, we suddenly realize who is really in our corner, and who is simply there to fill a need of theirs. Because our 'door' is letting people in, we open ourselves up to those who really do have our best interest at heart. The saying goes:

'If you hold onto grudges, you won't be able to catch your blessings'.

Unfortunately, we innately attract people who are have issues just like us, or issues that complement ours. For example, if you are defensive, you might find someone who builds walls up as well, another defensive person. The relationship will never grow to what it could be, because it's just two people scared to get hurt. Lies, dishonesty, distance, and lack of emotion keep the relationship stagnant, and eventually kills any chance of a real future. People who build walls are also likely to attract a 'compliment' to their defense. People who are wrecking balls, and destroy things. They use you, demean you, play on your insecurities, and shame you into doing what they

The Journey: Sunrise

want. This is also a form of defense. One that smothers you until there is no challenge to fight against. Either way, when you are in a defensive, insecure position, you can only attract people who are on your level of defense or lower. You have to begin to build doors instead of walls. No one can love you more than you have allowed them to. It is simply not possible. So if you choose to build a moat around your castle, don't expect to be saved. There are so many people waiting to help you build, you just have to start the work. The ones who are also in a good place, in a place of giving and more importantly, receiving love, will see where you are, and want to help build with you. And a relationship built on showing and receiving love, has a great foundation! Build more doors.

As we continue to build doors, we realize that they are not meant to be built by us alone. Someone is handing us materials, helping us sculpt and design these doors. We realize that this life, this human experience, is indeed a group one. It has been since birth. We are born into a gigantic melting pot of lives. Into an existing web of ideas, experiences, beliefs, and cultural influence. People. We are the glue that makes this experience what it is. And because of such, we can understand that nobody in this world is meant to be alone. In fact, isolating yourself, is the most harmful thing you can do to your psyche. You can begin to convince yourself that nobody cares or understands you, and begin to build those walls of defense. Until we realize that not only is life not about just us, but that we ourselves have been influenced by generations of people we have never even contemplated, we can feel so alone and lost.

Once we open ourselves up to the idea that there are so many people waiting to love you, waiting to help you, and so many people fighting for you right now, we can begin to tear down those walls and let them in. We can understand that many people have, and do, feel exactly how you do. People have been through what you have, felt the things you've felt, and can benefit from your story, and you theirs. Embrace the hardships that sculpted you, and use them to be exactly who you needed at that time. We are meant to connect with those people to help us on our Journey. We can exchange ideas, feelings, experiences, so we can begin to not feel so alone or misunderstood. We often times will fight to the death for our loved ones, but will not allow them to fight for us. Allow yourself to make mistakes and forgive yourself like you do for others. Allow yourself to cry and ask for help, and for someone to be there for you like you are for them. Allow yourself to say you don't know, and ask for clarity. Allow yourself to receive every ounce of love, passion, and creativity you have given to others. After-all, if you can do so much, and give so much love to other people, imagine how you could be loved. Try not to settle for less.

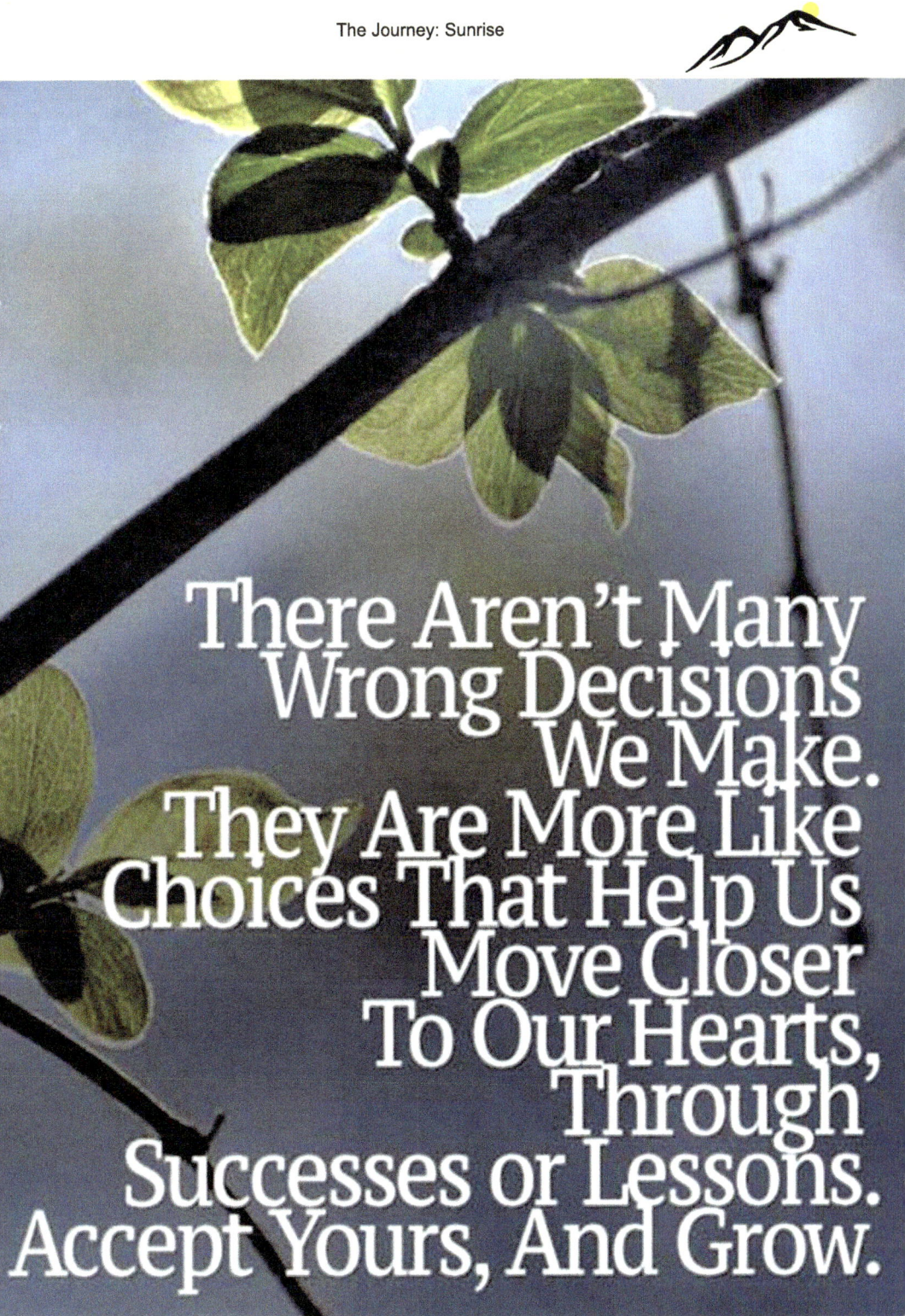

What is on your mind?

-10-

Mirrors

It is also important to realize that people are mirrors to us. It is very difficult for us to be completely objective as to who we are, especially on an ego, or subconscious, level. Even the most self aware individual will not be able to give a completely accurate assessment of him or herself. This is another reason why isolating ourselves is dangerous: people are our only mirrors into our ego. Understand that by no means does this mean that these people are perfect. I always give the example of a fun house at a carnival. If you had no clue what you looked like, and were sent into a fun house to figure it, how would it go? You might have an idea of what you look like, maybe an ideal image in your head. Upon entering, some mirrors would make you look super fat, others skinny. Some would give you a big head, others tiny feet. Some would make it hard to make out any detail at all. But in each mirror, you could find a detail. Hair color. Shirt color. Eye color. Skin color. Every mirror gives you a small piece to the puzzle until you have a good sense of how you really look. Our ego is this person, and the people we choose to surround ourselves with, the mirrors.

Most of us have an ideal image of ourselves in our head, and if left unchecked, we can believe fiercely it is who we are, and how we are perceived by others. But it is important to observe those around us, to reflect on comments made about us. It is important to reflect on conversations, even disagreements, and to glean even the smallest detail from it about ourselves. It is important to observe how we make others feel. This is part of taking personal responsibility. People are not perfect. They themselves have a lot of issues as well. Nobody is perfect. But just like the fun house, even though the reflection is not perfect, it can help us put together the full picture of who we are. Take time to reflect on the mirrors around you. Who we choose to reflect for us. Make sure the mirrors give an accurate reflection, and not a distorted one. It is important to surround yourself with like minded people, who all are striving to stay on the Journey as well. We can't grow in unnourished soil.

"If you show me your friends, I can show you your future"

-Mark Ambrose

The Journey: Sunrise

It is important to remember that some mirrors (or people, situations, and conversations), reveal a lot more than others, but they all are a reflection of ourselves, no matter how distorted, and it is important to continue to try to understand pieces our Ego, through others.

Take a good look at those around you, including your mate. They say that we are who we choose to associate with. We are naturally drawn to like-minded people, or people who compliment our insecurities. Those around us also reflect on our inner thoughts and emotions in a big way. Are they angry, violent, selfish, maybe distant? Are they loving, caring, supportive, and patient? Question your Ego on why you chose to be surrounded by these folks. Is it because you value yourself, and respect who you are, and therefore chose to align with others that do as well? Do you feel uncomfortable around positive people, not wanting to have a higher standard placed on you and your behavior by your friends? Are you proud to introduce them to others? Do you feel loved and supported by them? Do you want to control their behavior most of the time? These are the kind of questions that should be considered when looking at our inner circle of associates. Either way, who they are tells us who we chose to align with, and can speak volumes about our own insecurities, fears, or negative traits. It can also show us a more positive side of ourselves, if we choose to align with those who are understanding, patient, and appreciative. They tell a story about who we are, who we choose to be, and who we want to be. If you want to elevate your level of joy and happiness, surround yourself with people who are striving to do the same. After-all, if our friends are not helping us grow, and are only content with temporary enjoyment, we are not building anything. We are simply sitting on the sidelines to happiness, as those moving forward on their Journey pass us by. Misery loves company, and not change. Begin on your Journey, understanding that not everyone will be happy with your progress. Be strong enough to let go of those who are weighing you down. Those who make every step on the Journey as strenuous and painful as possible. Simply bettering yourself can speak volumes about our associates, and can show us who really loves us for us, or who loves us simply for the role we play in THEIR lives. Continue on YOUR Journey, fueling your own steps. Those who really cherish you, will cheer you on. The world needs you. The best you. Your talents, creativity, passion, and experiences are too valuable not to contribute. Be very careful who you choose to align yourself with. Be cognizant of your mirrors.

The Journey: Sunrise

"In life we go through phases. Only those who can transition with you, from your lowest point, to your most successful peak, will be left standing in the end. Some people are perfect for you. Friends, family, coworkers, lovers... but only at a certain time in your life."

What is on your mind?

-11-

Nothing Grows Without The Warm Rays of Love

All of this valuable information, although potentially complex, can be summed up into one statement: Nothing can grow (at least to its fullest potential) without unconditional love. Including you. This book teaches you how to find that inside yourself by filtering out all of the influences and experiences that were inherited from others. Things cannot grow under the effects of rage, regret, anger, sadness, etc. How many of those emotions feel familiar? When someone is angry, they refuse to listen to others, and will often argue. When someone is sad, they often cry, isolate themselves, become defensive, or can turn to vices such as food, gambling, drugs etc. Regret? Well that stops a lot of people from moving forward, into the future, because they are too busy trying to fix the past. All of these emotions have one thing in common: They STOP all growth, and keep us in the same place. Whether in our day to day, or from past experiences or childhood, these are the feelings that dominate most people's subconscious. For most of us, we were given these emotions from family, friends, entertainment and such. How many of us had or have parents that have issues with fears, insecurities, or other similar ideologies? These fears are then shared with us over and over again, especially in our younger years, and thus become apart of our subconscious. In a lot of ways, we are literally given certain emotions, feelings, and values. Some of them are beneficial. For example, looking both ways before you cross a street. How many of us find ourselves still using this principle well into our adult life? It was beat into our subconscious for years until it became automatic, fearing to cross even the most barren street before looking. We then pass this on to our kids. Similar to this, fears of people, places, or opportunities can be passed down.

Regrets can be passed down, tremendously affecting how we see the world. A great example, is a parent who never finished college (or maybe felt they never had the opportunity to attend). They may have dropped out, felt they weren't smart enough to go, didn't have the finances, had kids early. Maybe they simply feel it is important to have a degree in our society. They may even push for you to be a certain 'thing', or have a certain occupation, or religious position. They constantly drill into your head that they want you to go to college, no matter what. You grow up not wanting to disappoint them or lose their love, and so college becomes your goal as well, even though deep down you may want to simply get a job,

or join the Army, or sing and write. Maybe you simply do not want to attend at all. Even though attending college can lead to a more stable adulthood for many, this parental advice isn't necessarily ONLY for our benefit, but more so somebody's fear, or possible insecurity. If after a deep personal interest was taken in you, and the decision of secondary school was best for YOU, that's great! But if your path was written for you well before you could even walk, it may be cause for reflection. The world may be missing out on a gift, a rose that was never allowed to bloom.

It is important to reflect on our environments, and more importantly our guardians who raised us. You will find that a lot of negative traits were passed down to us. Not through genetics or inheritance, but through subconscious conditioning. It is important to release the control of these negative gifts from those around us, to tap into a more genuine, and happy you. Meditation, therapy, and books like these can help us decipher the complex code that makes us who we are, and begin to get rid of emotions and feelings we no longer wish to carry. If you find yourself feeling angry a lot, frustrated, sad, regretful, insecure, or feel that you are not good enough to do something, the answer probably lies in your experiences growing up, especially under the tutelage of your guardians. The more you examine your Ego, the more you will start to understand these feelings, how they were manifested in you, and you can begin to shed the weight of negative emotions, for a more positive, and peaceful life!

You will always have a broken Future
When you try to fix the Past
You can only truly heal in the Present

What is on your mind?

-12-

Given Permission to be Bigger

I speak with a lot people who are extremely frustrated with themselves about issues that they may not be able to move beyond. This can be especially true when it comes to a mate, friend, or even family. We may be frustrated that they repeat the same mistakes over and over again. These issues can range from anger, trust or honesty, to insecurities or commitment problems. Most of the time when we have disagreements with someone, it can get to a very emotionally charged point of no return. After all, when someone gets very angry, they will not be open to hearing or understanding much, as they are vehemently trying to prove their point. And therein lies the revelation: arguments (much different than general disagreements) stem from a person wanting the other person to understand how they feel. Simple as that. This is tough though, because we may have different values, thoughts, fears, emotions, logic, and so many other traits that differ from one person to the next. Getting someone to understand your viewpoint can be a battle within itself sometimes. But once again, it starts with us taking personal responsibility.

We should strive to first of all, to understand where the other person is coming from. What experiences have they had that might make them feel this way? How does their mind work about this topic? Are they educated on it? Do they TRULY understand how they feel, or are they just emotional right now? These are but a few examples of thoughts and questions we can ask ourselves about any argument or disagreement we have with folks. Trying to understand where they come from, even when we disagree very strongly, helps to move discussions, and thus energy and efforts, towards a solution and not a stalemate of ideologies. Even the most irrational argument can be understood if the effort is given. Remember, understanding is NOT agreeing! It is simply seeing things from their point of view. Once someone feels understood, they no longer have to try to prove anything, and a solution, or compromise, can begin to be worked on. Even if there is no real solution, at least the conversation can be productive in knowing how said person feels, thus giving you the choice of dealing with, or avoiding that particular topic or situation in the future. After all, we only have control over us. Trying to control a person's thoughts, or actions, only speaks to a lack of comfortability in self. So, if we can learn more about people around us, it only helps us to attract and indulge in situations that are favorable and positive for us. When dealing with people, you have two options: either accept them for who they are and leave, or accept them for who they are and chose to

The Journey: Sunrise

love them anyway. But either way, you have to accept them. If people or viewpoints are simply not agreeable, we can choose to either avoid those situations, or simply love someone for their differences, hopefully inspiring them to be better. Emotionally arguing a point is not productive, and only leads to us being stagnant, because once again, things can only grow with love.

Through this type of diffusion, often times people can see for themselves if they are being irrational, fearful, insecure, or have some other emotion influencing them. This is the goal. For people to see issues within themselves. This gives them the real chance of improving and growing. Although we can always point out flaws and help people, it seems to be much more effective if the conclusions are found by the person, within the person. Giving this understanding is giving love. Sometimes being truthful and honest about our own mistakes, allows people to feel comfortable with their own as well. It lets them know we are all flawed. Discussing our Journey and where we came from, also allows people to see that it is OK to be exactly where they are at, and consequently allows them to accept and give kindness to their own story. More of us should discuss the ugliest parts of us, to allow others to see the beauty in theirs. Your story is inspiring, and can help people on their Journey. Share your gift!

A lot of times people lash out in anger, simply as a

"When You Love Someone, *unconditionally,* even for their worst parts, you give them permission to be **bigger than they have allowed themselves to be.**"

-the Journey: Sunrise

defense mechanism. Often they are ashamed, angry, or insecure about something. Ego figures that they should bring the conversation to a negative point, and get a reaction out of you. This helps them to then deflect their frustrations onto you, and not have to deal with it internally. Not allowing yourself to stoop to a negative emotional level forces the person to take responsibility for their actions. Subsequently loving and accepting them for this, can be the breakthrough they really need for real change. We of course still can stand our ground in making a point we believe in, but expecting a change in someone can be dangerous, and thus lead to a stalemate. Again, if situations bother us to a point of bringing us to a negative point, perhaps evaluating why we chose to deal with these things (or how to accept them if we DO chose to associate with them) is the best course of action. We can only control ourselves. Choose your story, along with the characters and plot it contains.

Most of us grew up in households or environments in which we had different pressures and challenges. Maybe it was a religious household, an abusive parent, or simply a lack of personal interest in us. Either way they all create a situation in which we feel inadequate in a lot of ways. Many of us not realizing that is the case. We may feel not good enough in our job or relationship. We may be very, very hard on ourselves if we mess up or make a mistake. We may feel we are not pretty enough, or that we have to make the 'right'

choice all the time. We may even feel like we are not as good as someone else at doing something, and not attempt it ourselves. People feel these feelings all of the time, and they can spill over into our personal lives and relationships, even leading to self destructive behavior, sabotaging our own relationships with people who have terribly negative effects on our lives. Learning to understand someone is an amazing step to not only loving them, but allowing them to love themselves, and in turn, demand the same love from others. We often feel these feelings of inadequacy, simply because nobody has loved us unconditionally, even for our lowest lows, and even for our biggest flaws. We simply had things expected of us growing up, to feel loved. Expectations from other flawed people, so it is understandable to feel this way. We feel these things because if some of these negative emotions come out, we might be ashamed of falling short of those expectations. If we can learn to love people, and understand them, we send the message that we unconditionally love them, even when they aren't perfect. A feeling that most people have never felt. When you love someone unconditionally, even for their worst parts, you give them permission to be bigger than they have allowed themselves to be. Bigger than what they have been told, or have felt their entire lives. Now this doesn't mean that you have to deal with everything people throw your way. Again, you have the ultimate control and can decide to not be a part of something, but loving those who you choose to align with (with the knowledge that nobody is perfect), will open up the door to them actually loving themselves, in way they were never allowed to previously.

People often say they want to be a 'nice' or 'more positive person', but that really doesn't mean much. We are all everything that we desire to be, and if you let your inner you shine, you'll see that. What does that mean? Getting rid of all of these labels, barriers, and expectations that have been placed on us. We can then finally be whoever, and whatever is really trying to break through. For example, I've heard many people say, 'I just want to be a good wife/husband'. While the end goal of being an amazing companion is commendable, focusing on only one aspect of the complex person you are, can actually hinder you in your goal. You might try and clean more, cook more, and plan out date nights. But focusing your energies into these goals, might push you to be less independent. Maybe less creative in your personal life, or lack of time spent with friends. These things can stop, or slow down your personal growth, not allowing the relationship to continue to grow as well. Whereas if you choose to shed the pressure of being a 'good husband/wife', you might realize you enjoy other aspects of the relationship, and not cooking and cleaning. This can then be communicated and a compromise made, leading to a happier, more authentic you, and doing things with your spouse that

you truly enjoy, also making them happier and feel appreciated. Trying to be one thing, is what stops us from being everything. Finding out what we are 'trying' to be so we can start working to be a more genuine you, allows us to become who we want to be, leading to a happier, healthier existence. Also, this only attracts the things that make us happy and feel good, and not the negative things that put pressure and stress on us to be 'something' (even though the feeling might be familiar, possibly from childhood, or a relationship).

The point is, continue to be the best you, and everything else will align with that. Do not compromise yourself for any one situation or person, because it will ultimately lead to failure. The reason being, if you can't be you, and accepted for that, you are not truly meant to be there. You are meant to be the best you. You are meant to shine, and offer your passion and talents to the world, to make it a better place. If a situation or person stops you from being that, it is unnatural. You are fighting against yourself and against your potential to stay there. This means you are stopping your Journey, or slowing it down. Usually life keeps kicking your ass until you choose to fight for yourself. You are meant to continue on your Journey, finding others along the way. Those that you naturally encounter, and are meant to be in your life at that time. The weight you carry, however, is not meant to be there. Shed the weight of expectation.

The weight of untapped potential. Continue on your Journey, and let people and situations occur along the way, not stopping too long for any one person if they try to hinder you. If they do not want to continue with you, then it is probably not meant to be. It may hurt, but the pain of looking at your goals, but not moving towards them, hurts deeper. Keep moving forward. Always.

The Journey: Sunrise By Dominic Herron

Im Looking Forward To The Memories of Right Now

-Drake

What is on your mind?

-13-

Doing The Work

Although this book was written as a collection of things I have learned along my Journey, and provides some things to do and think about, ultimately the work will have to be done by you. Incorporating the things mentioned here into your life, with patience, and kindness, can help get you started on The Journey to your own peace and happiness. A true peace that negative circumstances that you encounter cannot steal. Meditation really helped me along the Journey. It's as simple as taking 10 minutes, closing your eyes, and counting your breaths. One on inhale, and one on exhale, to 10. Then repeat. This practice helps us to get in touch with our Ego, helping to see what it contains, and how it works. It is like watching a movie of our subconscious. We are not expected to do anything but observe. It not only helps us sort out what's important, but gives our minds a much needed break from the hectic pace we deal with everyday, especially in our culture. Therapy is a great tool as well. Getting a completely objective view of yourself and your thoughts, from a third party, can really help some people. Again, mirrors. Sometimes our family and friends can hold us to our old selves, and hinder our growth. Although they may have our best interests at heart, it is important to know that your change and growth will be challenging to others. Sometimes when we conquer things it brings out the insecurities or fears of others, simply because they might fear they are not able to beat the issues you have, or they want to keep you at their low level. Often they are scared to 'lose' you. Continue to fight to be the best you, and let The Law of Attraction weed out those who are not supportive of that. When you elevate, people around you have to either elevate themselves, or they will seek other people at their lower level, and slowly distance themselves from you. Either way, you win.

There are many ways in which books, speakers, or videos can help us on our Journey. Whatever resonates with you and your heart, use it. Whatever doesn't, don't bother. The point is, you have to do the work, and that work has to resonate within you. None of these things can save you, or give you exactly what you need. As difficult and emotional as it might be to face, as we discussed, the answers and peace you seek, are inside of you. It may take time to find it, and that is OK. Be patient, and have balance through the tough times. Once you have your own happiness, it's yours forever. The Journey is different for everyone, and yours is equally as unique. Embrace your story. Embrace every step, with patience and love. You will soon look back, and see how truly far you've come.

Life will feel lighter. You will be more positive and it will spill over to your family and friends. And that's what it's about, sharing our light with the world. When we all do, it becomes a better place. You have a story to tell. We are all on this Journey, and can help each other continue to move forward. Your Sunrise is only the beginning. Now that you are awake, it's time to get moving! Your heart is waiting to open to all of the people and places you will encounter. Your heart is waiting to be loved! Begin your Journey. And keep moving forward, even if it feels like you're 'Drifting': my next Journal.

Penned With Love,

Dominic Herron

What is on your mind?

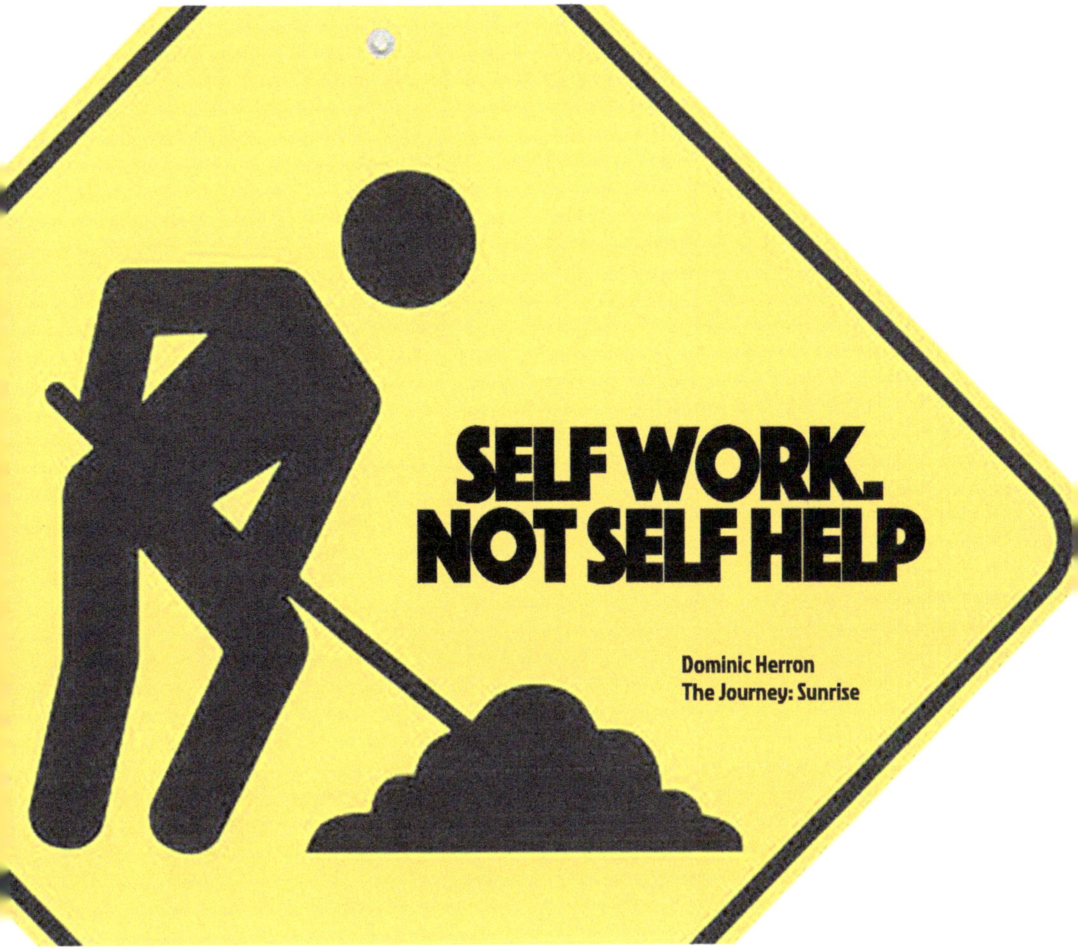
SELF WORK.
NOT SELF HELP
Dominic Herron
The Journey: Sunrise

Continue to move forward on your Journey.

Always...

The Journey: Sunrise

DRIFTING...

The Journey: Sunrise

The Journey: Sunrise

Acknowledgments

I would like to thank all of my friends and family that have pushed and inspired me along my Journey. I would like to thank my brother, Justin Herron, for always pushing me to big bigger and greater than I currently am. I would like to thank my mom Tracey Edwards and her husband Henry, for their advice and continuing support, and for giving their time to help me complete this body of work. I would also like to thank Megan Martin, a dear friend who has been a close companion in the completion of this body of work, as well as a gifted artist that helped with the production of 'The Journey'. Thank you to my dad Martino, and friend Marlon, for our conversations that also helped flesh out the material. Also thank you to my closest friends Kyle, Jorge, and Stephen, for the long talks, and the amazing life experiences that have lead me on my Journey. Thank you to my brother and sister Dante and Desiree as well for their support. Annette Rochelle Aben, for her fine editing job! And lastly, thank you to Blurb and Book Wright for being great tools to self publish my work, and allowing me to put out my thoughts and experiences in the way closest to my heart. I deeply thank you all, and I hope to continue my Journey in the best way possible, growing with you amazing souls along the way!

The Journey: Sunrise

About The Author

Dominic Herron is a serial entrepreneur from Ypsilanti, Michigan. His passion for changing lives compelled him to open his own successful Holistic Health business, The Grow Bar (TheGrowBar.com), in which he actively helps people in his community with physical, mental, and spiritual classes and products. He uses his unique life story and experiences, that includes growing up in the Jehovah's Witness faith, the loss of a young marriage, and dropping out of The University of Michigan, with a 'full ride' scholarship, to pursue his passion at 19, as resources to begin to help people on their own Journey to finding themselves, and success. His business, and mission have been featured in numerous articles, and newspapers including The Detroit Free Press and USA Today Network. With his extensive donations of resources and time, he has affected the lives of so many people across the country, speaking and inspiring people to find their own happiness. His years of experience helping people heal, from the inside and out, are presented in a simple, yet intuitive fashion, that is both engaging, and thought-provoking, whether speaking, or in published print.

Visit DominicHerron.com

The Journey: Sunrise

Every person you will ever meet, knows something you don't...

The Journey: Sunrise

The Journey: Sunrise

CPSIA information can be obtained
at www.ICGtesting.com
Printed in the USA
BVOW10*2243070717
488524BV00013B/49/P